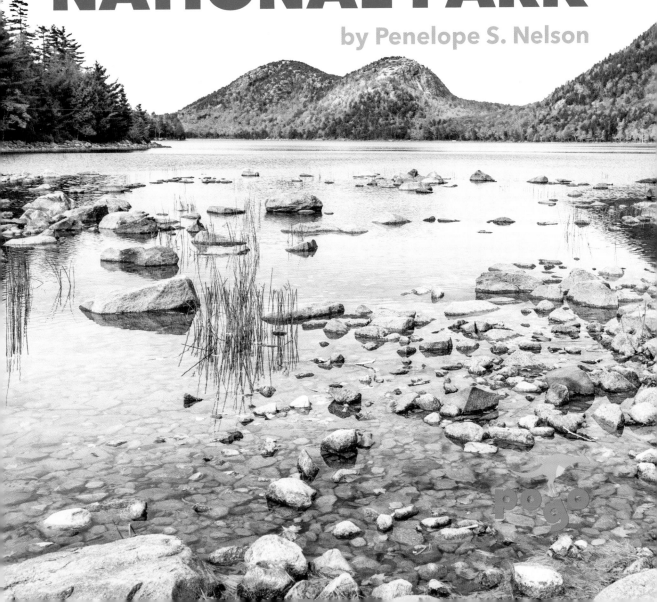

U.S. NATIONAL PARKS
ACADIA
NATIONAL PARK

by Penelope S. Nelson

Ideas for Parents and Teachers

Pogo Books let children practice reading informational text while introducing them to nonfiction features such as headings, labels, sidebars, maps, and diagrams, as well as a table of contents, glossary, and index.

Carefully leveled text with a strong photo match offers early fluent readers the support they need to succeed.

Before Reading

- "Walk" through the book and point out the various nonfiction features. Ask the student what purpose each feature serves.
- Look at the glossary together. Read and discuss the words.

Read the Book

- Have the child read the book independently.
- Invite him or her to list questions that arise from reading.

After Reading

- Discuss the child's questions. Talk about how he or she might find answers to those questions.
- Prompt the child to think more. Ask: Acadia National Park was started to keep the area safe from too much building. Is there a place that you would like to help keep safe from development?

Pogo Books are published by Jump!
5357 Penn Avenue South
Minneapolis, MN 55419
www.jumplibrary.com

Library of Congress Cataloging-in-Publication Data

Names: Nelson, Penelope, 1994-
Title: Acadia National Park / by Penelope S. Nelson.
Description: Minneapolis, MN: Jump!, 2020.
Series: U.S. National Parks | "Pogo Books."
Includes bibliographical references and index.
Identifiers: LCCN 2018050912 (print)
LCCN 2018052554 (ebook)
ISBN 9781641288088 (ebook)
ISBN 9781641288071 (hardcover : alk. paper)
Subjects: LCSH: Acadia National Park (Me.)
Juvenile literature.
Classification: LCC F27.M9 (ebook)
LCC F27.M9 N45 2020 (print)
DDC 974.1/45—dc23
LC record available at https://lccn.loc.gov/2018050912

Editor: Jenna Trnka
Designer: Jenna Casura

Photo Credits: Vlad G/Shutterstock, cover; Silvia Bianchini/iStock, 1, 6-7; Miro Vrlik Photography/Shutterstock, 3; BlueBarronPhoto/Shutterstock, 4; Lukas Proszowski/Shutterstock, 5; kickstand/iStock, 8; Pat & Chuck Blackley/Alamy, 9; Alessandro Oggioni/Shutterstock, 10-11; Michael Marquand/Getty, 12-13; PictureLake/iStock, 14; Carl D. Walsh/Aurora Open/SuperStock, 15; Mike Ver Sprill/Shutterstock, 16-17; BlueBarronPhoto/iStock, 18-19tl; Collins93/Shutterstock, 18-19tr; Terry Sohl/Alamy, 18-19bl; Harry Collins/Alamy, 18-19br; Jerry and Marcy Monkman/EcoPhotography.com/Alamy, 20-21; Bram Reusen/Shutterstock, 23.

Printed in the United States of America at Corporate Graphics in North Mankato, Minnesota.

TABLE OF CONTENTS

CHAPTER 1

A COASTAL TREASURE

Does exploring **tide pools** on the coast sound fun?

tide pool

Would you like to hike a mountain to watch the sun rise over the Atlantic Ocean? Cadillac Mountain is just the place! It is the highest point in Acadia National Park.

This park is on Maine's coast. It is made up of islands and a **peninsula**.

This area was made a national park in 1919. These are run by the U.S. government. The land is protected. So are the plants and animals that live here.

WHAT DO YOU THINK?

People **donated** the land for this national park. Why? They wanted to keep it safe from development. Why do you think people wanted to protect this area?

CHAPTER 2

MANY SIGHTS AND ECOSYSTEMS

Spot lighthouses during your visit. Bass Harbor Head Light flashes through the night sky.

Bass Harbor Head Light

Stone bridges cross streams, rivers, and roads. Old carriage roads wind through the park. Walk, bike, or ride horses on them. You can even ride a horse-drawn carriage!

carriage

The park has many **ecosystems**. Animals like moose, beavers, snakes, and turtles live in them. There are forests and lakes. There are many **wetlands**.

TAKE A LOOK!

Look at the **intertidal zone** below. At low tide, the water level is low in this zone. You can see tide pools and the creatures, like sea stars and crabs, that live in them.

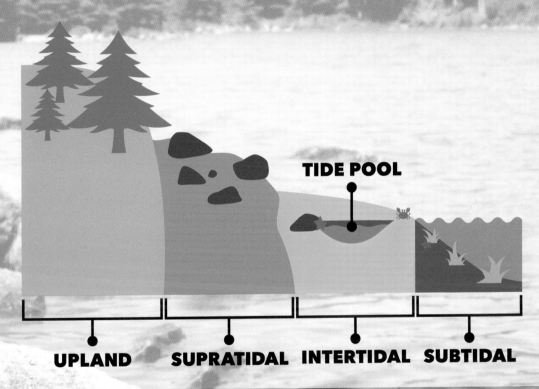

TIDE POOL

UPLAND   SUPRATIDAL   INTERTIDAL   SUBTIDAL

Thunder Hole

Mountains, beaches, and rocky shorelines are all **landforms** to see here. Listen to the sounds of Thunder Hole. Waves crash against the rocky **inlet**. Boom! It sounds like thunder!

DID YOU KNOW?

Glaciers formed across this area more than 9,000 years ago! They moved and exposed rock. They created the park's many lakes and valleys.

CHAPTER 3

EXPLORE THE PARK

Take to the trails! Some wind down the coast. Others go through the forests. More go up the mountains. Trails run along the park's many lakes. Jordan Pond is actually a lake. It is 150 feet (46 meters) deep!

Jordan Pond

The **climate** here changes with every season. Summers are hot. Winters are cold and snowy. Some trails are open all year. In the winter, you can cross-country ski, snowmobile, or ice fish.

Drive along Park Loop Road. It winds through Mount Desert Island. You can camp here! Pitch a tent. Spend the night on this busy island.

You can camp on Isle au Haut, too. You must take a **ferry** to get to this island.

Enjoy stargazing! Clear skies reveal the stars. You could see the **Milky Way**!

Milky Way

sandpiper

loon

warbler

peregrine falcon

Do you like bird-watching? Ship Harbor Trail is a great place to spot birds. More than 300 **species** are in this park. You could see sandpipers, loons, warblers, and even peregrine falcons! These birds nest in the Jordan Cliffs.

WHAT DO YOU THINK?

Peregrine falcons were once **endangered**. The park helped bring them back. Some park trails close when chicks are hatching. How do you think this helps?

Head to the shore. Sand Beach is a great place to swim. You can see the Beehive here. It is a rocky **peak** people hike and rock climb!

Acadia National Park is a beautiful place! What would you like to see first?

Beehive

Sand Beach

QUICK FACTS & TOOLS

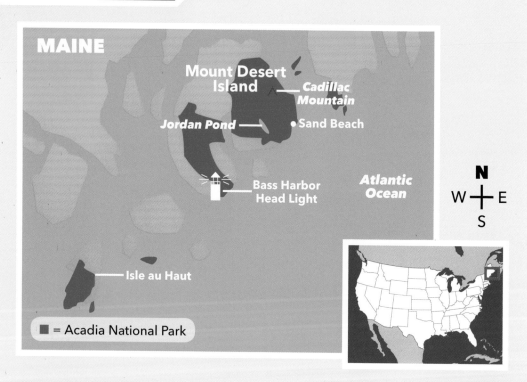

MAINE

Mount Desert Island

Cadillac Mountain

Jordan Pond

Sand Beach

Bass Harbor Head Light

Atlantic Ocean

Isle au Haut

■ = Acadia National Park

ACADIA NATIONAL PARK

Location: Maine

Year Established: 1919

Area: 47,000 acres (19,020 hectares)

Approximate Yearly Visitors: 2.5 million

Top Attractions: Cadillac Mountain, Jordan Pond, Sand Beach

GLOSSARY

climate: The weather typical of a place over a long period of time.

donated: Gave something to a charity or cause.

ecosystems: Areas that include all of the living and nonliving things within them.

endangered: In danger of becoming extinct.

ferry: A boat that regularly carries people across a body of water.

glaciers: Large, slow-moving masses of ice.

inlet: A narrow body of water that leads inland from a larger body of water, such as an ocean.

intertidal zone: The area along the shoreline that is above water at low tide and underwater at high tide.

landforms: Natural features of land surfaces.

Milky Way: The galaxy that includes our solar system and more than 100 billion stars and appears as a white streak in the night sky.

peak: The pointed top of a high mountain.

peninsula: A piece of land that sticks out from a larger landmass and is almost completely surrounded by water.

species: One of the groups into which similar animals and plants are divided.

tide pools: Shallow pools in an intertidal zone that often contain sea creatures.

wetlands: Marshy and wet areas of land.

TO LEARN MORE

Finding more information is as easy as 1, 2, 3.

❶ Go to www.factsurfer.com

❷ Enter "AcadiaNationalPark" into the search box.

❸ Choose your book to see a list of websites.

FACT SURFER